ACTIN

Scal

for Margaret,
  and the resilience
  of mothers

'The most beautiful part of your body
is where it's headed.'
           Ocean Vuong

ISBN: 978-1-913642-39-6

The author has asserted their right to be identified as the author of this Work in accordance with the Copyright, Designs and Patents Act 1988

Book designed by Aaron Kent

Edited by Aaron Kent

Broken Sleep Books (2021), Talgarreg, Wales

Contents

Neil Gilks, 'Seen It All', 2020, courtesy of the artist.

Acting Out

Peter Scalpello

after us,

                        there was
a boy from romania. fingertips itching i ran
through his densely tousled crown that bore
fragments of a political self-derision. escaping
through the mouth his tongue tapped
upon sorrow, my kisses between drags of a
shared roll-up in the doorway that held us in
a moment of conjecture.

            there was gus. he was nice & uncertain
            of how to exploit it, his form a thick stem
            budding up out from the dancefloor of the gay
            club where we had our first date. funny, he had
            on a football shirt (i don't know what team) as if
            it testified to manhood, or something. in him
            i recognised a rationale for sexual currency
            assigned to 'straight acting'; a make-believe
            acceptance to one's singular expression of gender.
            the irrelevance of it all. we partied
            an eliminated seduction among tourists from happier
            places, got carried away, carried
            out the building.

            after gus there was
            a boy from germany. we didn't date.
            his eyes dulled with virescent intent,
            which i stared into while giving him
            head. deep in the pupils, they seemed to say
            i have a girlfriend.
            he blocked me on whatsapp after
            & i didn't hear from him again.

kindness

when did i stop being kind to you
& why did I do that?
                    I found you
on vauxhall bridge signalling
you were about to
           jump.
                clinging on
to you i sensed
           you folding in
        on yourself like the feelers
of a mimosa plant when
        touched.

when did I stop being?
                kind to you &
why did i?   do that
               we passed on
the street as my brow crumpled
                  in
sight of you, two boys frowning
      at each other to express their
          desire.
intentions on a periphery; to fuck
                or fight.

when did i stop being fuck to you & why
did I fight that? i don't cope well
               with being
oppressed, You said.   you remind me
of how not to be   a dominator.

                why
did I stop being   kind to you? &
when? did i do that
            I couldn't tell you
the last time i let a scab
          just heal by itself.

open doors

(i)

i do this for my family, hustle like / they'd kill me if they knew it, which / is likely. my son is eight. or, he / was eight, then i left. lives with / my mother now, in our home / country. the choice was mine & / i came here to work, for him. make / his future hopeful, to enable life. / investment & sacrifice, they're the same / thing. & graft i do. urban exposure / makes a spatial gaze, to be hyperaware. / though my intentions tire in bare legs; / it's 03:15.

(we)

universal credit doesn't exist for us / unrecognised by sedate society. but to its / husbands, we're on shift. he watches me trot, / all street-based survival & so; / i'm working. simply i cannot afford / the cost of living in this city & / my english, not so good. so i crawl / the kerbs, taking tariffs in left / hands. tempered engines giggle on / approach, a joyful dread, though i'm / not a criminal. hair stiffens at my nape, i / pull & twist at its tuft. i won't grovel. / waving to no one: *he's just taking / down your plate number.*

(you)

endurance is a lifted scab. i am / the opposite of institutionalised; / this precarious / nocturne is all for you. recurrent cycle / more a progressive outward spiral, / to our shared destination. to reach you / taller, well-fed. & proud of your mother.

as a boy
it seemed that grown-ups

all lacked a history,
always had been rooted

in that particular
phase of being; never

an earlier iteration
existed, they were in

fact impossibly final.
constraints of my developmental

understanding allowed not for
insights of past failure, the friends

& lovers abandoned,
acts of spite & vulnerable

ego. in my naivety
an adult was made whole, a wholly

unflappable significance.
as such i learned not to

question the authoritative
demand. subservient

to benchmarked maturity,
i avoided persecution

by conditioned compliance,
hoping one day i too

would possess the strength to swing
a punch like that,

provoke fear with loud noises
from the heady window glare.

like a grown-up.

amid the spectacle of masculinity
        i also grew into one. watch me

            raise my voice, these knuckles
                that are decibels. dare you

                    interpret me as anything other?
                        i've matured now, just look

                        at my stance.

                                    i don't believe
                                in the supremacy of adulthood

                            anymore. confessional
                        dominance has changed

                        my biology,

                    now i see you as
                the inner child, second chance

                at an imperfect genesis.
            embrace me

            with an upward glance,
        your soul is made pure

        from exposure to the finite.
    please take me

        for what i am; every man
    is a memory

    of birth.

reunion

i want to be in glasgow
slumped against brick
that scuffs away a tattoo of you from my exposed back

i want to be in london
sat in the soot
pinching fingertips at city workers for fifty pence, please

i want to be in london
changing my cells
if you find me let us speak the language of forgiveness

i want to be in glasgow
holding a fag
to front teeth that skew the symmetry of my smile

The New Viral Sensation

'Hell ain't things lasting forever. Hell is change.'
Toni Morrison

14

Fail to learn from the deformity of previous generations
& we ultimately put future society at risk, warns
the recording of a human voice, rendered now
through a podcast i touched from the invisible cloud
The words transition a significance towards my current
predicament, though the topic of conversation was:
gender binaries
At this circadian axis you could be fooled
into thinking that nothing was out of the ordinary,
tilted as i am
Splodges of life bleed a condensation visage; the window
i daren't open
Boring my eyes into the density of light, willing
residents of the homogeneous high-rise opposite to show
themselves, i watch as they flicker on & off, one at a time
Calls to mind the drawl of you, words a viscous
rationality: it wouldn't be (isn't) fair (on me) to go on
(your opinion) like this (dysfunctional) it's (definitely)
not your (my) fault (but) maybe (what) if you (i) weren't
so easy-going (you controlling) all the time (passive)
The clearest exit is my phone screen; blocking
your number would be a self-imposed quarantine
Everything everywhere else continues /

13

I am fed on the newsfeed
It tells me once the germ slips inside a building it can
track you up the halls & under the gap of your
door, down the air vents & through
your bathroom piping
Up to now i've still been using the toilet, but
assuring the lid's down from when i flush it
'til i'm sat there again
I don't wash my hands at all /

12

I've switched the air conditioning off at the wall
& stuffed the doorframe with anything i could
find under the sink
Help urself to whatevrs in fridge, the owner
messaged, so i slosh their chardonnay into a mug & take
pictures of myself, pick the one i look most symmetrical
in & upload it, captioned *still alive lol*
I don't drink any as i wait & glare as my view
count rises
The feed says it can live & grow in cupboards
& on foodstuffs for a fortnight, longer, before you even
notice it
I lunge for the window in an attempt to eradicate
the mug, before recalling my air seclusion, & instead
conceal it in a chest of drawers stuffed with socks
i'll never be able to wear again /

11

In the last place, i'd bought three litre-bottles
of organic vodka as a souvenir for my sister, but
that i'd assumed we'd drink together
I reason them safe if drunk straight from
the fiery lip, letting each sip flutter at my own
vacant mouth
Wincing, heaving, it makes my blood glow
Days pass like this, vomit in the sink i can't wash
away /

9

The clean heat of severance increases; i've taken to
wearing nothing but my pants, phone attached to
the plugpoint at all times, battery fattening
I imagine it getting in through the facelike
slits of the socket, a smirking invasion i had allowed
Gaze still fixed to the handset, i blow the room with
silver, organism or machine /

8

The more layers i have on, the more protected i am,
that's science
I am swallowed by the sofa, filming updates for others;
the dull exertion of a thumb
Through the screen i'm handed many citrine symbols
of varying distress for my dewy pixelar outline,
shivering from the heat & surrounded by borrowed space
I massive-sneeze & am so startled by it, i sob,
but no one else can see it, so i stop
I realise that i am starving /

7

I receive a message from my sister, it is a video
of a screen playing a video
In it, a man in a tight suit raises his right hand
to a virtual congregation demanding answers;
my eyes twitch involuntarily, make clicking noises
when i blink
With ambiguous authority, the man assures that
a vaccine can be developed in sixteen days
He is outside of the city, glittering from blue light
& he is safe
It's gone viral, my sister says, meaning the video
Even under the circumstances we still have a laugh /

6

I've been surviving on tins of tuna & baked beans
chewed cold from their ring-pull rim, letting the sweet
juices converse in my jaw to create their own
unique entity, which drips across my chin & dots
the carpet
I rub it all in & wash it down with the vodka, pressing
my cheeks like the depression of computer keys
Periodically i'll throw up, laughing into the porcelain
bowl i've stopped flushing
I've stopped masturbating, too; heightened
promiscuity an alleged sign of the illness,
even in straight people
#VirilityEqualsVirality
Something is broken /

5

The apartment owner tries ringing me & i decline
the call, cackling
I check the hashtags in search of someone like me,
dammed & thirsting for digital connection,
but there's only outraged people on the other side
of the planet
A chorus of keyboard egos informs me that nearby
tenants have fled from indoors to seek refuge
in the vastness of the city, a freedom afforded
only to those who risk exposure for a pinnacle
of urban catharsis
I could never be that fucking brave /

4

I've started using the vodka to wash my hands, my face
I'm cleaner than i've ever been
I miss you /

3

The man in the suit says they're close
to vaccine distribution, just consulting pharmaceutical
conglomerates now
The hospital has had to close because the staff
all got sick
I don't go near the window anymore
Everyone everywhere else is outraged
Why won't you text me? /

2 days ago

Dancing in & out of sleep like a sedative, the walls
no longer white, my phone no longer plugged in
You are looking up at me
with that smile you always had, like you're amused
by something & not paying attention to me
It is a dream
In it, you are the virus physically embodied
I keep moving towards you, i can smell you & want you
to smell me; i stink of shit & paint-stripper
The closer i get, the smaller you become,
so indistinct & yet thoroughly yourself, calling out
that i want you, & be with me, & you just say

i shouldn't come near you, it's (definitely)
not safe, it wouldn't be (isn't) fair /

Yesterday
I wake to so many missed calls i just turn off
my phone & launch it across the room, banging
fists against the walls, shouting HELLO
in all the languages i can think of & invent,
& i'm panting, retching, weeping into the plaster,
red as the silence in my ears,
knotted in reverie among empty tuna cans,
& suddenly inside them, backstroking through
utopian brine oceans, sealed off from molecules
of doubt, craving to be touched,
skin slick with sweat, snot, & all
i can think about is you,
the virus, you, &
outside: the perpetual sun /

Today
I am the weakest, the maddest, whistling
my favourite song as if asphyxiated, just hissing
Bathroom stench fills the space around me like
a misdiagnosis, & i need out of these clothes
The building is infected, of this much now i'm certain,
tearing apart my charger to keep the socket plugged
& the voices out
The phone is dead, that is to say it serves only
as a reflector to my isolation, which is always the case
actually
I lick condensation from the window glass, gasping
for the slightest hydration, to be purified
I spread my tongue across both panes & think of you,
the marks i make, concentric prayers
Peering out, i witness the street like it's the first time
i've ever known such composition: the altitudes
of concrete, parallel lives, pavements
scant & granite
& there's a person, solo, ambling
through the middle of the road, where cars would
usually fester

The person glances up, around, & doesn't recognise
me; so far under, alone in the world
that is entirely theirs
Fail to learn from the deformity of previous generations
& we ultimately put future society at risk, i think
as i disrobe, the odour so potent that i dissociate
from correlation to my own body
I blast through the apartment
 & unstick the door
  hurling myself towards the elevator
   legs fizzing &
    unable toc oordina temovem ent
    slamming into the walls
     & breathing in everything
      i click the elevator button four times
       humming & bouncing as adrenaline
       obliteratesmyperipheries
        in our descent to ground
         swaggering towards the exit
          at its threshold i realise
           i've been screaming the whole way down
           I stop, cover my mouth,
            step outside /

The stillness is immaculate.

flagging

i'm not addicted
to tina i'm addicted
to destroying myself

i used to meet men
at bars but
i can't drink anymore
  & the pubs have all closed

    ankles & toes
        steeped in deviancy i
            am the lone wolf fucking
    in the forest

  when i'm yawning
for filler like
sock cuffs
don't call me daddy

when you're flagging tell me
  twice

roof top

clenched balls
of my feet   climbing
steel getaway   a ladder out
of ourselves   i followed
him up &   out surrounded
by circles   when we
reached the top he   giggled
that we could   witness
the city   & truly be
together   in dimness & the
cold pinch   of him at my
waist we dangled   legs &
trainers   were thick with
masquerade   i took his
gaze with me   to the
precipice &   shook
myself out over   the edge
listened as my   piss
sugared the trees   agape
he came   up & held
on until   i couldn't
exhale myself   anymore &
denied impulse   just blew
bits of lung   tissue at the
view until   our hearts stopped
racing &   he texted who
did you send that smirk
face to it wasn't
me

tend
er

oppressed &
hypersexual,
i

question
what's the
link

between
violence &
homoero

ticism as the
boiler churns.

you fucking
love me &
say

it again,
hard knuckle

my back so
sheets
dampen in

taps to the
romance of

sacrifice. the
rumour of

sobriety
allows no
ritual, so

our love is
not default.

my tiny
existence this

headstand &
tongue with

your dna.
carry it like

rainwater
weighs down
the

river, like we
get all dress

ed up &
then can't
leave

the house.
how can you
say

love so much
although i'm

not enough?
how can

don't tell
anyone mean

that was all
i've ever

dreamed of

split

my therapist	told me to
separate 'the thought'	from 'the feeling'
& so i	intend to
sever the memory	of you
lips at the gutter	kissing your sick
into the concrete	outside
our building	yale abandoned
giddy	in park bushes
from	the pleasure of my
escapist reflex	eastpak weighted
with your score	parcels
i hollowed into	the river
splits the park	bushes &
the feeling	from thoughts of
the ways we used to punish each other	
&	ourselves

outed

sun rising   i didn't particularly   want to   but i let him
inside me   all flesh & bone & appetite   adult bodies made
of childhood wounds   we tried we   trawled through netflix
to find one without   an outed abusive male   actor as protagonist
isn't possible   he said   text the dealer   so i hit 'hi da—   it
predicts   'hi daddy'   & my thumbs stain sly   from app use
are we *Discreet* ?   we take drugs because   it's fun   &
because we can   he says   he thinks he likes cocaine too
much   & meth too   much   painkiller   never again   he says
he thinks he likes straight guys   more 'cause   that's who
traumatised him   called him   sissy   says it didn't seem
a problem when they were fucking him   always asks
high   "am i a good boy?"   ask yourself   that   three ridges
the rim of his ear   an

ellipsis   a warning   ash   in his hair   dew   under his nose

you were a trance   song played through   dying speakers
broke out   the box you were   left in &   i
became your   new box   emptied out like   pigeon shit
pavement constellations   comments on porn
sites disclose abuse   & comments like   "that's hot"
like prelude   to a sneeze
tragedies give people a pass   to behave horribly but
i was not committed   to it   how would it
feel to be touched
by grace

ode to tracksuit

my hungered polyester   thighs show you no
mercy   if you can even fathom
my shape through all   this rustle

what happened to
your levi's, dude

remember when we used
to sport these bottoms   as a uniform
as   armour against ridicule

we grew out of this   didn't we
remember when   we donned matching shell suits
& drank   cider from three-litre containers
that served us almost everything   we needed
to be able to swallow
our attractions & get with   the girls by the river
between dregs forming   fag holes

i know you
remember when we ruined   our friendship
by circling the inside of each
other's cheeks with   underdeveloped tongues

the rub of that nothing
fabric was like   touching skin & my
crotch in activewear could keep
nothing secret

now you   jog up to me in dalston
with the same leaden legs
that fled from teenage   shame panting
for what i guess is   reclamation or subversion or
both things   but in the form
of an easily removable manliness

remember when we donned
matching shell suits &   were happy
to be invisible

take off   your trackies & show
me what hasn't
changed underneath

fruit bowl

a guy at work narrates to me his hamartia) he recounts
that one day last year he'd smoked crystal) & had sex
fourteen times with about eight) different people off an
app) he came down with syphilis & now has to limit
himself) it's five a day for a reason, he said) after he's
finished reflecting, i take) myself to the staff bathroom)
to pee) at the urinal i consider my penis & suddenly i'm)
repulsed by it, like my anatomy specifically) represents a
cumulative suffering) my strange antenna, the sum of all
man's compulsion) i put my dick back & sit chastely at
my desk for the) rest of the afternoon; a body with a
penis, observing) the trials of others with the same)
surely enlightened, i question which is an addiction)

which is an addiction ?

when i was in two
bodies, halved

insisting on life i dressed
myselves up, like a wound

as a bigger me, older & more engendered
than i am even now
though, then, i of course
defied age & sex

my father's masculine was anger
i first gauged as urges indulged

to etch, as caveperson
the letter ⑧ with
a (nondescript) wrench, made up
of roughened integers so

erasure shaped our liminal space
& the inside of his testicles read *sis*

let's say the impulse
to deface already had
infinite rotational symmetry
it seems to surface in me today

screaming on regents street
at the injustices of the world

my mother's feminine was doubt
i sensed in her primary colours
& her venus, which is the name
of a razor i took to both eyebrows

though barely there & now
vanished, replaced them with

love hearts; sky, sun, wine
but the security, i could literally inhale
it! i was untarnished & fine
& when i looked back up i was already

                    here
                                when i was two people, doubled

        everything served
                                        disappeared down
my throat until the suburbs
                    brought it all back up again

    with seven pints of revelation
                    to ingest the suede shoes

            & the unwell man you see all the time
                                        is you
                    both cells unmarried & yet
                            a replication, as healing

            means to be repeatedly broken over again
                                        when
                    fingertips were viscous

        & not-yet yellowed, the matter of us
                    tasted so gorgeous—
are you coming with me, or just

                            merely going

begin again

                            when i was in two

chem & other poems

Scalpello

for Conor,
  for everything

  'I am always writing my pamphlet of abuse poems'
              Richard Scott

ISBN: 978-1-913642-39-6

The author has asserted their right to be identified as the author of this Work in accordance with the Copyright, Designs and Patents Act 1988

Book designed by Aaron Kent

Edited by Aaron Kent

Broken Sleep Books (2021), Talgarreg, Wales

Contents

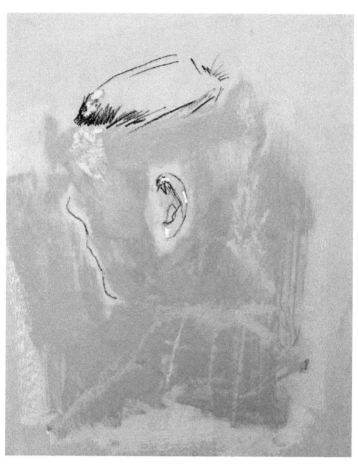

Neil Gilks, 'Bus of Shame', 2020, courtesy of the artist.

chem & other poems

Peter Scalpello

little soy sauce fish bottle
        fixed with GBL,
                pleasure buds an unbound nozzle
                        spouts vitreous, a miniscule relief

invisible, really   squeeze down
            your eager thumbs &
                        was it even there?

                    what's 2ml to
                            man, tattoos that score the width
                                of a heaving torso

                            one lucid bream to ravage
                                inhibition, subdue
                                    dysfunction, arrest
                                     your forever fervent
                                aorta,

                            arrest forever your—

                        little zesty puddle of
                    impetus, distilled

        we drop we do it with
         irony

what i don't talk about

*'I remember saying no to things that
happened anyway'*
Jamila Woods

picture this: you are sat opposite your abuser,
have arranged it. inhale
& the universe
applauds. don't hear it.

makes looking & to touch
with transference a radical act
of self-disclosure, though commonly known.
makes you illuminated.

squinting through
aerosol eyes, you are ignited
in light of the past.
it flickers.

do you regret/rescind/or   even
recall the form of whom
you seized?
              all of your hands
that peeled a former skin
which held the void,   our
formative dysfunctions.

assert as you asserted that
i am not your victim.
for were we not
born equal;

                                        pith

everywhere?

pass it on

i don't know who it was.

from the lapse in time, an interval which
defined, thus a lapse in also judgement,
i could speculate ~ a set of
clenching shoulders, freckled from burn ~

his inner thighs, angled in longing ~
the sting of your beard, abrasive unto
my grimacing cheek ~ a feeling
of presence, motion that declares he is there,
so then i am here, too.

no, i don't know who it was,

& yet i concede the relevance
of certainty, for are we not cumulative; a seed
surely provoked by proximity, so willingly
invaded, to receive quota of a shared grief?

reciprocal bite made
unique, our cellular rivalry
has domesticated. i ponder you now,
faceless clone ~ baring mutual insignia,
how to each other we

remain unknown.

status

blood samples. three pulsing vials.
torrent, exhale, trickle.
have you heard of prep? i mean
emtricitabine…tenofovir, i mean
descovy, truvada?

trials. paris, cameroon, cambodia.
i wept for us, as blood performed
an act of betrayal. the fire inside
445mg moves me forward.
what have we learned?

to prick. a caring kind of violence.
dismantle my fingerprint, snatch out
my sins. consume & declare them on
cotton, pure, stain
a shameful crimson.

my sins, which you put there
with disinfected hands, absolved i
play a hand in absolution.
guarded façades remain
asymptomatic.

with trembling fists blindfold me, unhinge
my jaw & fill it with
truvada. each pill a sapphire relief.
give me one for every soul i ever held inside
me,
every [▓▓] i [▓▓] this year.

so cram me full, breach capacity
until i choke on my own salvation.
you upped the price & we bled. i spread
my whole & was fed
another chance, for another

chest, his arms & thighs
that grip my need. still i bleed.
my status. why
deny me this armour,
molecular affinity?

how could i outrun
what has been prescribed to me

Sex and drugs often go
hand in hand – they have done
for decades [1]

It all started when I
was out with my friends [2]

Of course, drink and drugs play a part
in the sex lives of many Brits [3]

A Gilead Sciences funded study
has found that HIV-positive men in England
are 'more likely to use chemsex drugs'
than other European countries [4]

the trio of substances
synonymous with chemsex – crystal meth,
GHB (also known as
the 'date rape' drug) and mephedrone [3]

They go out for drinks on a Friday night and tumble
down a chemsex rabbit hole from which
they don't emerge till Monday, or later [3]

When taken, GBL is converted into GHB inside
the body and produces feelings of euphoria
and reduced inhibitions for up to seven hours,
meaning it is commonly associated with group sex [5]

How worried should we be? [6]

"At the end of the day who wouldn't
like to fuck like a porn star, fuck
for two or three days?" [1]

Moral panics often focus
around drug use and non-traditional
sexualities, so it's tempting to dismiss
the scaremongering around chemsex
as precisely that [6]

"This is not the same
as having sex after a few glasses of wine" [3]

He still wanted to explore
his sexual interest in men but was lost
about how to do so outside
the context of drug use [3]

The UK is experiencing a "significant" increase
in patients seeking therapy for 'sober sex' [3]

amid a £200m health cut [7]

the margin for error is
so small [3]

[1] Ryan, Ó. (2018), 'How one drug can make sex euphoric, but also destroy lives', *TheJournal.ie*

[2] Hanjabam, S. (2019), 'I Lost Myself to India's Chemsex Scene and Overdosed, but Survived to Tell the Story', *VICE*

[3] Gallagher, S. (2019), 'Chemsex Comedown: What's Behind The Rise In People Seeking Therapy For Sober Sex', *HuffPost UK*

[4] Kelleher, P. (2019), 'HIV-positive men in England 'more likely to use chemsex drugs' than other European countries, study finds', *PinkNews*

[5] Munro, V. (2018), 'South London 'chemsex' drug gang caught when police found parcel of GBL', *Croydon Advertiser*

[6] Speed, B. (2016), 'What is chemsex? And how worried should we be?', *New Statesman*

[7] Flynn, P. (2015), 'Addicted to chemsex: 'It's a horror story'', *The Guardian*

chem

G	meph	more	more
		GBL	

			crystal
G	meph	than	meth
		crys	

		tal	than
G	meph	meth	G

body of a toddler wakes to find not
its father where he'd lain as routine

i don't anymore but at the time
i thought it was adequate to long
for sexual connections & romantic
gratification & project that
ambition onto regular interactions
with men on the internet or in person
to achieve validation

this speculative kinship led me to you

bedroom disquieted
a gradient of sleepy hues   moonlit punctures
through curtain cast upon unconcerned furniture
*   he is not there*

we met at somebody's basement flat
a vision of gentrification
you came with whatsername
i didn't know anything
about you but i'd seen your profile
& that was affirmation enough
in person you were even better
looking & though i wanted to
right away i left it
a while before i made my move
offered you my
mephedrone laced with de-wormer
you seemed happy just
to sip your bud & i too
quenched metaphorical thirst but
you said sure & trusted
the ambiguous powder my door key
to oblivion & to i hoped your desire

brazen curiosity conquers terror & leads you
to the hallway   lone & unaccustomed to night
*   -time when murkiness*
of the hour alludes to secrecy   towards the lodger's

you were charismatic & so fucking handsome
i tried to mirror your allure to appear
nonchalant but just nodded a lot & laughed
when it seemed i was expected to
really i was gone by this point & only
wanted to blink at your stubble &
prep-blue eyes
your gregarious smirk & nicked tooth
said you chipped it as a teenager chewing
lids off of beer bottles & scar tissue
above your left eye socket as
testament to a facial modification
outgrown

room   slowed movements   a hazy sojourn
    unfathomable sonance
pervades from within you see an image
defined in dusk they are   on the bed

submissive to social approval i continued sniffing
with you & sucking roll-ups like a hand down
my throat when you went back inside for
a minute to see if your friend was alright my flatmate
came over & said they'd heard you're into pretty
out-there sex stuff & i faked like i was
maybe down for that too as i tremored in the daisies
squeezing a tobacco pouch that depicted someone lying
in foetal position among sterile bedsheets

it kind of looked like me

you spoke of the first relationship with a man
you were seventeen & he forty-three
a corporate type & not out
initially the thrill was boundless the
precarious dynamic satisfied a vacant
dominance you believed sexuality
capable of relieving
liberation came in the split following
a proliferation of enforced group sex
of which you were keynote
migratory impulse in heartbreak led
you to solo-travelling
archetypal passage from west to east
in search of depth & authentic self
found
in bangkok a gay sauna
a nostalgia
the same men but on your terms

i sensed your disclosure as manifest
of our entanglement & so
reciprocated

i recounted how in secondary school i befriended
in the negligent sense a guy
in his fifties whom i met on an internet chatroom
for gay people his thin eyebrows
a whisper opposing the stiff upper lip of a
bushy moustache cast upon incognito browser
my own bareness reflected in his semi-
ironic spectacles
he had a kind smile
& grateful energy so i went
'round his house once a week sometimes
he wanted me to suck him off but mostly
i just kept him company
in the months we served each other
i discovered what it meant to be wanted & he
allowed
soon he lost the glasses
started wearing dual diamond-stud earrings
& found someone else
fresher than i

& how i endeavoured in the suppressive sense
in heterosexuality experimented
with expectation upon the opposite
sex against better judgement
it was an era
of attempted eradication to my
deviant desires & at times
i even achieved the normative assumption
persuaded myself
a tendency for the womanly when
it was i ascribed to the shameful effeminate
certitude provided short-lived
restoration with the futile notion
of divine cure of correction
yet despite amorality of then self
i still exist
on favourability

different skin joined
at the same middle   the act
develops as you

we were an effortless dilation
& the hours accelerated
i drew hands taut against the sharp
dome of a skull freshly shorn
controlled & pure
your teeth at my neck pleading
a territorial command & crotch
grabs loaded with intemperance
in the backseat of a prius
we were practically neighbours
& in my abbreviated state
i sussed this as omnipotent
intent so surrendered myself
to the erotics of fate

call out

you led me descending
stone to a doorway that advised obligation
i indulged cumulative proximity
& chemical nerve to galvanise
a performed assurance of motive
your mattress arthritic upon the
encroaching crimson carpet
expressions of predestination implicated a kindling
adrenaline extraneous to lust but in fact
apprehension
horizontal i reasoned the dichotomy
of coveted pleasure & just wanting to cuddle
that confused craving for intimacy
could we just hug for a minute i said as our noses
touched to behold but a freudian blur

or was it
could you get me a drink?
you tucked your erection to the groin
of your jeans & left for rum &
ice a pipe & a pipette
of G i slumped
across the bedroom wall back bare
& sweaty my peripheral form
clinging to the affected
gloss of a photograph

depicted   was   a   young   boy
in   the   lap   of   a   radiant   woman
captured   in   profile   their   gaze
upon   each   other   mouths   akin
pouted   to   express   a   virginal   kiss   an   impossible
bond   it   was   very   sweet   who's   that
said   aloud   to   no   one
eyelids   licking   themselves   to   savour
the   promise   of   immaculate   affinity
with   another   of   something   higher
&   more   &
i   passed

out

that night in your bed i dreamt i was a curlew
my bill a slender downturned rind

heart pure   intentions soft   & wings
overwrought with escapist desire

with beady bird eyes i beheld their plumage   lamented
as feathers were plucked from my extremities

by invisible force   each quill whistled in its departure
a sedative displacement

my hide eventually settles atop the shallow channel
fluid to its tide   thriving   away

sapphire   teal &   perfect indigo
lost

for decades

drink and drugs

inside
the body

Moral   s often

lost

I

play a part

in

chemsex

converted into

a porn star

for

a   cut

Of course

the trio of substances

on a Friday night

produce   feelings of euphoria
and

At the end of the day

it's tempting

after a few glasses of wine

to explore
men

amid

the margin   s

I

a   m

scare   d

of

sober sex

'you're

gay

be

cause

of

what

hap

pened

to

you'

choose your own sequence

a fact of nature
is to test the boundaries of
any new setting

as a body of
water reaches its threshold
to be comforted

the ruptured vein of
my inner elbow is a
curious molehill

my liquid lover
gushes for me to test our
sad perimeter

on the same street we
first met he walks right past me
after we'd fucked twice

face down i figured
out then you have to bury
your dead really good

now i'm at the point
where i can forgive myself
for swallowing pills

each day fluid calls
to mind that life is short but
living can be long

life gave me lust &
what i've got to show for it
is all this lustre

my adapted self
at the chillout gurning on
anti-depressants

32

'*I don't want to stop but it's time*
For therapy.'
                    Ariana Reines

Acknowledgements

Many thanks are due to the generous editors of the following journals and anthologies, in which some of these poems first appeared: Cipher Shorts, Consilience, fourteen poems, Fruit Journal, Gutter, harana poetry, perverse, Places of Poetry, a queer anthology of wilderness, Sonic Boom, Under the Radar, and Untitled: Voices.

Thanks to Kostya, for publishing me first.

Thank you to my editor and publisher, Aaron, for believing in these pamphlets. I'm grateful for your expertise and kindness through everything. Thanks also to Charlie and the whole Broken Sleep family, for their company, support, and writing.

Thanks to Neil Gilks (Neilsecluded) for contributing his artwork.

For their feedback and encouragement, I'd like to thank Mary Jean, Will, Richard, Danez, Andrew, Seán, Niven, Mícheál, Serge, Ewan, Helen, Natalie, both Michaels, Megan, Hannah, Rebecca, Leah, Chris, Torben, Adam, Brian, Gabriel, Robin, Bethany, Gavin, Ollie, Jamie, Tim, Katie, Freya, Yash, Connie, Amy, Tom, Gary, Wayne, and Suna.

For their inspiration and support, I'd like to thank Aimee, Ellie, Bernie, Jim, Robbie, Lewis, Liam, Edem, Rosalie, Julia, Monica, Caitlin, Emily, Cathleen, Seren, Kevin, Rachael, Day, and Brendan.

Thank you to my patients and colleagues in sexual health and HIV care, who inspire me daily.

For the attendees and organisers of HIV/AIDS in the 21st Century: Memorialisation, Representation and Temporality at University of Manchester, thank you.

Thanks to Liverpool Queer Poetry Collective for having me, and for their light in the lead-up to this publication.

For the readers and booksellers, thank you.

To the Keappock-De Ceapóg-Roes, for their love and enthusiasm.

To my mum, with love. Please don't read this.

To Conor, you mean the world.

LAY OUT YOUR UNREST

LAY OUT YOUR UNREST

Acknowledgements

The epigraphs are from 'Someday I'll Love Ocean Vuong' by Ocean Vuong, 'Permissions' by Richard Scott, 'SONIA' by Jamila Woods, 'Sula' by Toni Morrison, and 'Open Fifths' by Ariana Reines.

'when i was in two/ bodies, halved' borrows and alters a lyric from 'Polly' by Moses Sumney.

Thank you to these artists, for their work and influence.

'status' was longlisted for the Show Me Yours Prize.

'The New Viral Sensation' was written speculatively in January 2020. It was shortlisted for the Creative Future Writers' Award, and longlisted for the Desperate Literature Short Fiction Prize.

Thank you to the judges of these prizes.